The 1930's: Painting & Sculpture in America

by William C. Agee

Whitney Museum of American Art, New York

October 15 · December 1, 1968

Copyright © 1968 by the Whitney Museum of American Art, New York
Designed by Susan Draper Tundisi
Printed in the United States of America
by Publishers Printing-Admiral Press, Inc., New York
Library of Congress Catalog Card Number: 68-57216

Acknowledgments

The initiative for my present study of the 1930's was provided by the project The New Deal and the Arts, a nationwide survey of the government programs of assistance to the arts during the period, which I directed for the Archives of American Art in 1964-65 under a grant from the Ford Foundation. I would first like to express my deep gratitude to both institutions for the opportunity which led to this exhibition and the accompanying catalogue. To those who worked with me on this project go my warmest thanks for the innumerable ways in which they have assisted me in gathering documentation.

On behalf of the Whitney Museum of American Art, I would like to thank the lenders who without fail have given so generously to the exhibition. Many of them have gone to considerable trouble and have made special exceptions in order to bring to the exhibition work of unusual importance to the art of the 1930's.

It would be impossible to thank adequately all those who in various ways have contributed to the exhibition at the many stages of its preparation. However, I would like to pay a special debt of gratitude to Lloyd Goodrich, Advisory Director of the Whitney Museum. Although our views and interpretations have frequently been at sharp variance, I have profited enormously from his wealth of knowledge, his publications which are in many cases the backbone of the 1930's literature, and above all from the challenge of his thinking which has forced me to examine the probity of mine at every turn.

Lastly, I must acknowledge the help of Mrs. Dudley Del Balso in the initial stages of the exhibition, and of Mrs. Sara Austen who has since overseen and guided the endless details of the exhibition and catalogue with infinite patience and skill.

Lenders

Mr. Josef Albers, New Haven, Connecticut
Mr. Ivan Albright, Woodstock, Vermont
Mr. Emil J. Arnold, New York
Mrs. Milton Avery, New York
The Baltimore Museum of Art
Mr. and Mrs. E. A. Bergman, Chicago, Illinois
Grace Borgenicht Gallery, New York
Dr. and Mrs. Irving F. Burton, Huntington Woods,
    Michigan
Mr. Giorgio Cavallon, New York
Cincinnati Art Museum
Mr. William N. Copley, New York
Cordier & Ekstrom, Inc., New York
Miss Dorothy Dehner, New York
Mrs. Burgoyne Diller, Atlantic Highlands,
    New Jersey
The Downtown Gallery, New York
Mr. John Ferren, New York
Forum Gallery, New York
Mr. Benjamin F. Garber, Cross River, New York
Mr. Fritz Glarner, Huntington, New York
Graham Gallery, Ltd., New York
Mr. Balcomb Greene, Montauk Point, New York
The Estate of George Grosz, Princeton,
    New Jersey
The Solomon R. Guggenheim Museum, New York
Mrs. Carol Ely Harper, Seattle, Washington
High Museum Art Association, Atlanta
Estate of Hans Hofmann, New York
Mr. Harry Holtzman, Old Lyme, Connecticut
Indiana University Museum of Art, Bloomington
Mr. Philip Johnson, New Canaan, Connecticut
Mr. Willem de Kooning, East Hampton, New York
William H. Lane Foundation, Leominster,
    Massachusetts
Mr. Ibram Lassaw, East Hampton, New York
The Mattatuck Museum, Waterbury, Connecticut
Mr. George McNeil, Brooklyn, New York
Mr. James Merrill, Stonington, Connecticut

The Metropolitan Museum of Art, New York
University of Minnesota Art Gallery, Minneapolis
The Minneapolis Institute of Arts
The Museum of Modern Art, New York
National Collection of Fine Arts,
    Smithsonian Institution, Washington, D. C.
Mr. and Mrs. Roy R. Neuberger, New York
The Pennsylvania Academy of the Fine Arts,
    Philadelphia
Perls Galleries, New York
Mr. and Mrs. Laughlin Phillips, Washington, D. C.
Mrs. Lee Krasner Pollock, courtesy of
    Marlborough-Gerson Galleries, Inc., New York
Private Collections, New York
Mrs. Rita Reinhardt, New York
Rose Art Museum, Brandeis University, Waltham,
    Massachusetts
City Art Museum of St. Louis
San Francisco Museum of Art
Mrs. Margarete Schultz, Great Neck, New York
The Estate of David Smith, courtesy of
    Marlborough-Gerson Galleries, Inc., New York
Mr. James Thrall Soby, New Canaan, Connecticut
Estate of Joseph Stella, courtesy of Robert
    Schoelkopf Gallery, New York
Mr. and Mrs. Windsor Utley, Seattle, Washington
Mr. and Mrs. Baltus B. Van Kleeck, Jr., Red Hook,
    New York
Mr. Chauncey L. Waddell, New York
Wadsworth Atheneum, Hartford, Connecticut
Willard Gallery, New York
Yale University Art Gallery, New Haven

The 1930's:
Painting and Sculpture in America

The turbulent forces of the 1930's — the Great Depression, the rise of Fascism and the approaching war, radical politics — so dominated the period that we have assumed the art of the thirties was almost exclusively "socially conscious" in response. Numerous artists were indeed involved with creating an art reflecting the social and political ferment in which they lived, as were others seeking an "art of the people" by portraying the heartland of their native America.

Yet this was only one aspect of American art in the thirties. Other artists, although in the minority and virtually unknown (art history is never determined by numbers, only by quality) were working in ways divorced from the political and social currents of the time. Many of them were, however, passionately involved with contemporary issues and events. Many attached a revolutionary interpretation to their art and saw it as an act of social change although they were committed to abstract art. They are equally men of their times and belong equally to the art of the period even though their art was not conceived as a direct instrument of political action. Far from being completely dominated by Regionalism, American Scene and Social Protest painting as most easy generalizations would have it, the thirties were in fact a rich and infinitely complex period. It is a watershed, the point at which old issues and problems met with the newer currents that were to emerge in the great flowering of American art after 1945.

Almost never considered in appraisals of the thirties is the older generation — those born in 1885 or before — which consisted of the artists who in the main were responsible for the first wave of modernism in this country prior to 1920. Yet they did not stop painting for the duration. On the contrary, artists as familiar as Sheeler, Dove, O'Keeffe and Marin, or as forgotten as Bruce, Storrs and Friedman, were at the very peak of their powers during the period. Their accomplishments are among the finest of the thirties, although they have nothing to do with politics, and immediately indicate that the period was far more complex than has been supposed.

The Social Protest, Regionalist and American Scene painters were part of a generation that reacted both here and in Europe against what they felt was the excessively private and remote cubist and cubist-derived abstraction of 1914. Like the European Dadaists and Surrealists — who were also for the most part born in the 1890's — the Social Protest and American Scene painters desired to reintegrate art more closely with life in terms that would more directly incorporate man's common experiences. Their art was both the cause and result of a more pervasive reaction against modernism in America which reflected the country's isolationist mood after 1920.

Social Protest, Regionalist and American Scene painting were the three paths the demand for a "socially conscious" art followed, all of which reached their point of highest concentration in the thirties. It is a mistake, however, to suppose, as is usually done, that they were "movements" in any sense of the word or that they were "born" in the thirties. American Scene painting, of which Regionalism is a geographic subdivision, has a long history in the 19th and 20th centuries. The distinguishing characteristics of thirties American Scene painting were well-defined by Burchfield and Benton by the mid-twenties. Social Protest painting really began with Dada in Berlin in 1919-21. George Grosz, a leading member of the Berlin group, transplanted its spirit to the United States when he came here in 1932. The work of the Mexican muralists Orozco and Rivera in the twenties also provided a major impetus to Social Protest painting. It is important to keep this historical background in mind if we are to understand that the thirties was not a monolithic period, either stylistically or conceptually.

Surrealism and Magic Realism attracted a great deal of attention in the United States during the thirties. The first wave of American artists drawn to the movement — Man Ray, Joseph Cornell, Peter Blume, Ivan Albright and Louis Guglielmi — concentrated almost exclusively on the "dream image," rendered in a photographic realism, that formed one pole of Surrealist art. The "abstract" phase of Surrealism, which derived from Breton's conception of psychic-automatism, never created a body of painting per se in this country in the thirties. Rather, its forms, techniques and attitudes were adapted in generalized ways in the late thirties and forties by those artists who reached their full maturity after World War II. Vital to the development of Surrealism in this country was the long line of artists such as Dali, Tanguy, Matta, Tchelitchew and others who either visited, or who stayed here for extended periods.

The tradition of Russian Constructivism and Dutch de Stijl, which merged at the Bauhaus, also made an important imprint on abstract art in America. At the time of his arrival here in 1933, Josef Albers, although not thought of as a "thirties artist," was producing work of superb quality. His teachings were widely influential in spreading the principles of a non-objective art based on a clarity and strict economy of structure, volume and color. Mondrian's work was known here in the early thirties and had a decisive and immediate effect on Burgoyne Diller and Harry Holtzman. Balcomb Greene, first chairman of the American Abstract Artists, founded in 1936, as well as Fritz Glarner and Ilya Bolotowsky, both members of the group, also produced "structural" abstractions.

What might be termed Precisionist Abstraction — marked by sharp formal delineations and hard, flat colors and derived from Synthetic Cubism, Léger and Hélion — accounted for a considerable segment of painting in the thirties. The brilliant abstractions of the garish American urban landscape done by Stuart

Davis, the advancing and receding forms of John Ferren and the optical sensations in the work of the young Ad Reinhardt should all be considered in this context.

At the same time, a more painterly and expressionist vein was rapidly developing under the influence of Matisse, Cubism, Miró, and Surrealism. It can be traced in the work of Milton Avery, Arshile Gorky, Hans Hofmann, Mark Tobey, Willem de Kooning, Jackson Pollock, George McNeil, Karl Knaths and John Graham. These artists are included in this exhibition, and must be considered as an integral part of the thirties, not because they became well-known at a later date, but because they were all strong artists whose work of the thirties stands on its own.

Sculpture in America began the decade in an impoverished state and entered the forties with a glowing promise, and is thus emblematic of the dynamic shifts within the thirties that belie the one-sided assumptions about the period. The ranking master of American sculpture until his death in 1935, Gaston Lachaise was perhaps the only figurative sculptor who could embody his deepest and most personal emotions in a consistently inventive and convincing art. Other artists of the figurative tradition, such as Hugo Robus, William Zorach and John Flannagan, sought a more indirect and symbolic content which would convey principles of birth, the stages of life and the regeneration of the spirit. By this symbolism, as well as through the highly-polished volumes of Robus and the direct carve and truth-to-materials methods of Zorach and Flannagan, thirties sculpture demonstrated its profound debt to Brancusi.

From 1915 until the early thirties, the only American to keep alive the possibility of an abstract sculpture was John Storrs, all but unknown today, but vitally important nevertheless. Thereafter, a younger generation of Americans began the path that was to fulfill the promise held out for sculpture by the methods of Cubism and Constructivism. By 1932, Alexander Calder had produced his first motorized, free-standing sculptures and by 1934 had done a series of suspended mobiles which contained all the wit and lyricism that has characterized his art ever since. At the same time, Joseph Cornell was creating the objects and boxes that mark him as the most personal and poetic of any Surrealist-influenced American. By the late thirties, Ibram Lassaw had effectively adapted the biomorphic, floating shapes of abstract surrealism to the cage enclosures related to Giacometti's sculpture. David Smith, whose importance to the thirties has been missed both then and now, also learned from Giacometti and most importantly, from the welded iron sculpture of Picasso and Gonzales. Although it still bears strong evidence of its debts, Smith's sculpture at this time is exhilarating for the unmistakable strength that later established his position as the greatest of all American sculptors.

No study of the thirties can ignore the momentous influence exerted by vanguard European artists. It is one of the paradoxes of the time that a period generally considered totally isolationist learned so much from Picasso, Matisse, Miró and Léger, and found therein the basis for a new and original art. The primary European source for Americans looking to the mainstream of modern art was Picasso, although he was not here; Matisse, almost as influential, only made one brief visit. Léger, however, was in this country in 1931, 1935, 1938-39 and 1940-46. Not only was his presence a stimulating force, but he in turn was deeply affected by the pace and texture of American life and at points virtually became an American in outlook and spirit. American art was infinitely enriched by those who came and stayed: Grosz, Albers, Glarner, Berman, Tanguy; by those who stayed for extended periods: Matta, Hélion, and Tchelitchew, as well as Léger; and by those such as Dali who briefly visited. Their arrival here prefaced the great influx of the forties — Mondrian, Ernst, Lipchitz, Masson and others, to whom one can trace in part the change of artistic climate in America.

The present exhibition is not conceived with any notions of sentiment, nostalgia or camp in mind, but solely in the belief that the thirties represent a crucial and far more complex chapter in our history than most would have it. Furthermore, far from being the dreary aesthetic stepchild of American art as the thirties is usually conceived, the period can boast of a high level of accomplishment in which we can trace, whatever we have conceived art to be, the roots that have shaped the course of our art.

[An extended essay on the 1930's will be published shortly in hard cover by Frederick A. Praeger, Inc. for the Whitney Museum of American Art.]

opposite:
Walt Kuhn.
The Blue Clown. 1931.
Oil on canvas. 30 x 25.
Collection Whitney Museum of American Art.

The Older Generation

opposite:
Arthur G. Dove.
Ferry Boat Wreck. 1931.
Oil on canvas. 18 x 30.
Collection Whitney Museum of American Art,
    Gift of Mr. and Mrs. Roy R. Neuberger (and purchase).

below:
Arthur G. Dove.
Sunrise, I. 1937.
Oil on canvas. 25 x 35.
Lent by William H. Lane Foundation.

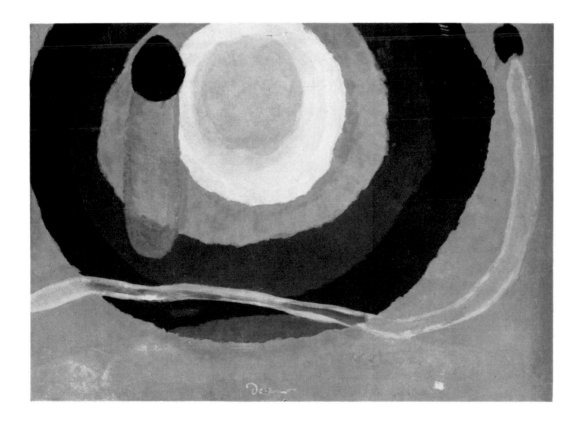

above:
Charles Demuth.
Buildings, Lancaster. 1930.
Oil on composition board. 24 x 20.
Collection Whitney Museum of American Art,
    Anonymous gift.

left:
Charles Sheeler.
River Rouge Plant. 1932.
Oil on canvas. 20 x 24⅛.
Collection Whitney Museum of American Art.

opposite:
Oscar Bluemner.
A Situation in Yellow. c. 1933.
Oil on canvas. 36 x 50½.
Collection Whitney Museum of American Art,
    Gift of Mr. and Mrs. Harry L. Koenigsberg.

right:
Georgia O'Keeffe.
Black, White and Blue. 1930.
Oil on canvas. 48 x 30.
Lent by The Downtown Gallery Collection.

opposite:
Georgia O'Keeffe.
Deer's Skull with Pedernal. 1936.
Oil on canvas. 36 x 30.
Lent by William H. Lane Foundation.

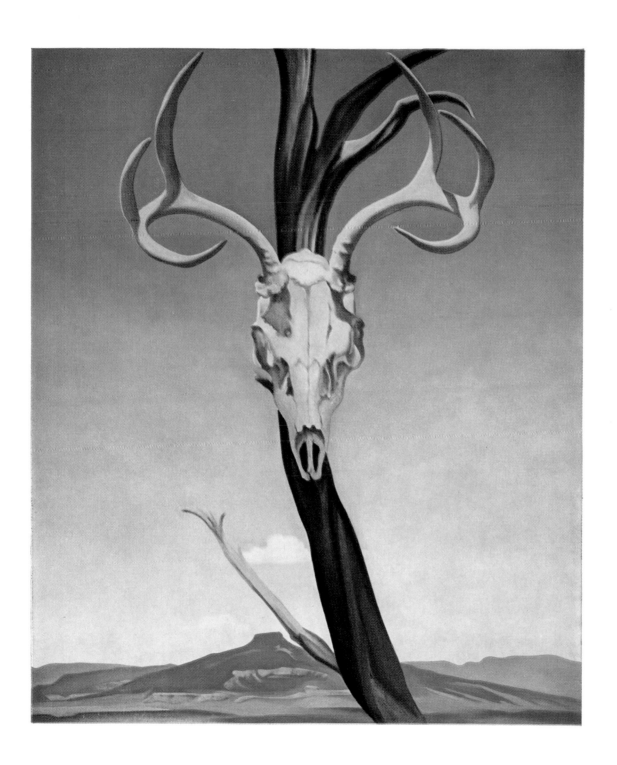

opposite:
Arthur B. Carles.
Composition. 1937-40.
Oil on canvas. 54½ x 67.
Private Collection.

left:
John Marin.
Region of Brooklyn Bridge Fantasy. 1932.
Watercolor. 18¾ x 22¼.
Collection Whitney Museum of American Art.

below:
John Marin.
Sea After Hurricane, Cape Split, Maine. 1938.
Oil on canvas. 23 x 30.
Lent by San Francisco Museum of Art,
    Gift of Mrs. Henry Potter Russell.

opposite:
Patrick Henry Bruce.
Forms. c. 1929-30.
Oil on canvas. 23¼ x 36.
Lent by Benjamin F. Garber.

below left:
Joseph Stella.
Bird and Tree. c. 1938-40.
Oil on canvas. 53 x 32.
Lent by the Stella Estate, courtesy of Robert
    Schoelkopf Gallery, New York.

below right:
John Storrs.
Abstract I. 1932.
Oil on canvas. 58 x 45.
Lent by The Downtown Gallery.

above:
Augustus Vincent Tack.
Before Egypt. c. 1930-35.
Oil on canvas mounted on composition board.
    Canvas: 16¾ x 36½; board: 26 x 45.
Collection Whitney Museum of American Art,
    Gift of Duncan Phillips.

opposite:
Marsden Hartley.
Eight Bells' Folly: Memorial for Hart Crane. 1933.
Oil on canvas. 31⅝ x 39⅜.
Lent by University of Minnesota Art Gallery,
    Gift of Ione and Hudson D. Walker, 1960.

Social Protest, American Scene and Regionalism

above:
Jack Levine.
String Quartette. 1934-37.
Tempera and oil on composition board. 47½ x 67½.
Lent by The Metropolitan Museum of Art,
    Arthur H. Hearn Fund, 1942.

opposite:
Ben Shahn.
The Passion of Sacco and Vanzetti. (1931-32).
    From the Sacco-Vanzetti series of 23 paintings.
Tempera on canvas. 84½ x 48.
Collection Whitney Museum of American Art,
    Gift of Edith and Milton Lowenthal
    in memory of Juliana Force.

above:
George Grosz.
Nazi Justice. 1937.
Watercolor and ink on paper. 19⅜ x 25.
Lent by High Museum Art Association.

opposite:
George Grosz.
A Piece of My World, II. c. 1938.
Oil on canvas. 39½ x 65.
Lent by the Estate of George Grosz.

above:
Raphael Soyer.
The Flower Vendor. 1935. (Repainted 1940).
Oil on canvas. 30 x 36.
Lent by Emil J. Arnold.

opposite above:
Grant Wood.
Daughters of Revolution. 1937.
Oil on panel. 20 x 40.
Lent by Cincinnati Art Museum.

opposite below:
William Gropper.
Art Patrons. 1939.
Oil on canvas. 15¼ x 21¾.
Lent by City Art Museum of St. Louis.

opposite:
Edward Hopper.
Early Sunday Morning. 1930.
Oil on canvas. 35 x 60.
Collection Whitney Museum of American Art.

below:
Edward Hopper.
New York Movie. 1939.
Oil on canvas. 32¼ x 40⅛.
Lent by The Museum of Modern Art, New York,
    Given anonymously, 1941.

opposite above:
John Steuart Curry.
Wisconsin Landscape. 1938-39.
Oil on canvas. 42 x 84.
Lent by The Metropolitan Museum of Art,
    George A. Hearn Fund, 1942.

opposite below:
Thomas Hart Benton.
Cradling Wheat. 1938.
Oil on canvas. 31 x 38.
Lent by City Art Museum of St. Louis.

below:
Reginald Marsh.
Twenty-Cent Movie. 1936.
Egg tempera on composition board. 30 x 40.
Collection Whitney Museum of American Art.

opposite:
Charles Burchfield.
Black Iron. 1935.
Watercolor. 29 x 41.
Lent by Dr. and Mrs. Irving F. Burton.

below:
Charles Burchfield.
Old House by Creek. 1932-38.
Oil on canvas. 34½ x 57.
Collection Whitney Museum of American Art.

Surrealism and Magic Realism

above:
Peter Blume.
The Eternal City. 1934-37.
Oil on canvas. 34 x 47⅞.
Lent by The Museum of Modern Art, New York,
   Mrs. Simon Guggenheim Fund, 1942.

opposite:
Ivan Albright.
And God Created Man in His Own Image. 1930-31.
Oil on canvas. 48 x 26.
Lent by the artist.

above:
Eugene Berman.
The Gates of the City, Nightfall. 1937.
Oil on canvas. 30¼ x 40¼.
Lent by The Museum of Modern Art, New York,
   Gift of James Thrall Soby, 1947.

opposite:
Philip Evergood.
Lily and the Sparrows. 1939.
Oil on composition board. 30 x 24.
Collection Whitney Museum of American Art.

opposite above:
Fédérico Castellon.
The Dark Figure. 1938.
Oil on canvas. 17 x 26⅛.
Collection Whitney Museum of American Art.

opposite below:
Edwin Dickinson.
Finger Lakes. 1935.
Oil on canvas. 23½ x 28½.
Lent by Chauncey L. Waddell.

below right:
Louis Guglielmi.
Isaac Walton in Brooklyn. 1937.
Oil on composition board. 29¾ x 23⅞.
Lent by The Museum of Modern Art, New York, Extended
    loan from the United States WPA Program, 1939.

below:
Kaye Sage.
My Room Has Two Doors. 1939.
Oil on canvas. 39 x 32.
Lent by The Mattatuck Museum.

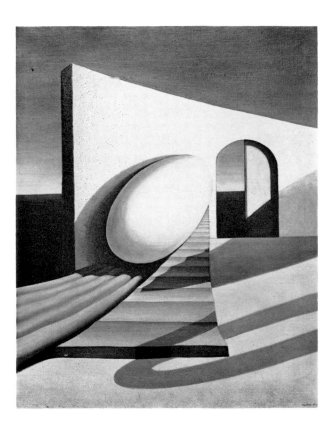

above:
Man Ray.
Observatory Time — The Lovers. 1932-34.
Oil on canvas. 39⅜ x 98½.
Lent by William N. Copley.

opposite:
Man Ray.
Le Beau Temps. 1939.
Oil on canvas. 112 x 108.
Lent by Cordier & Ekstrom, Inc.

Structural Abstraction

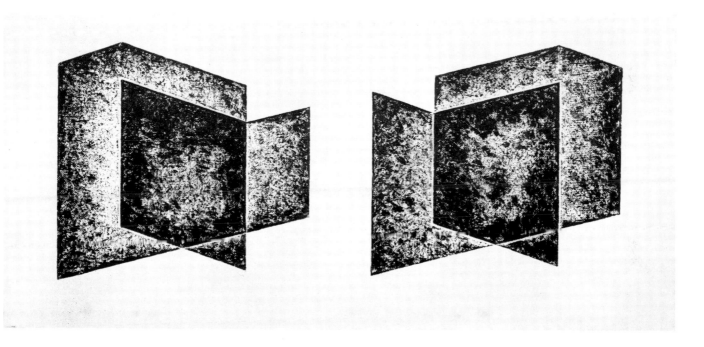

above:
Josef Albers.
Equal and Unequal. 1939.
Oil on masonite. 19 x 43.
Lent by the artist.

opposite:
Josef Albers.
Movement in Gray. 1939.
Oil on masonite. 36 x 35.
Lent by the artist.

opposite:
Jean Xceron.
Composition Number 242. 1937.
Oil on canvas. 45⅞ x 31⅞.
Lent by The Solomon R. Guggenheim Museum, New York.

below left:
Burgoyne Diller.
First Theme. 1933-34.
Oil on canvas. 30 x 30.
Lent by Mrs. Burgoyne Diller.

below right:
Burgoyne Diller.
Second Theme. 1938.
Oil on canvas. 34 x 34.
Lent by Mrs. Burgoyne Diller.

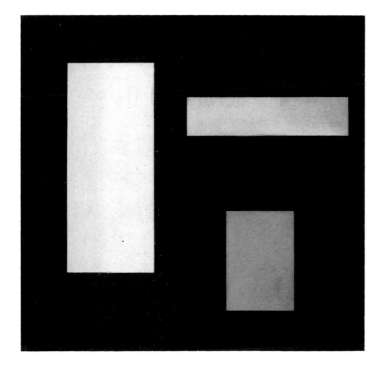

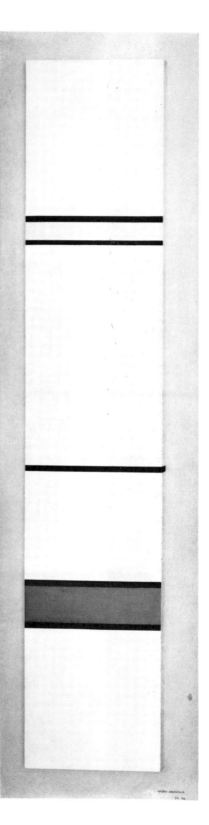

opposite left:
Balcomb Greene.
Green Composition. 1938.
Oil on masonite. 14½ x 22½.
Lent by the artist.

opposite right:
Harry Holtzman.
Vertical Volume, Number 1. 1939-40.
Oil and casein on gesso on masonite. 60 x 12.
Lent by the artist.

left:
Ilya Bolotowsky.
White Abstraction. 1934-35.
Oil on canvas. 36¾ x 19.
Lent by Grace Borgenicht Gallery.

above:
László Moholy-Nagy.
Space Modulator. 1938-40.
Oil on canvas. 47 x 47.
Collection Whitney Museum of American Art,
 Gift of Mrs. Sibyl Moholy-Nagy.

opposite:
Fritz Glarner.
Painting. 1937.
Oil on canvas. 45 x 56.
Lent by the artist.

Precisionist Abstraction

opposite:
George L. K. Morris.
Stockbridge Church. 1935.
Oil on canvas. 54 x 45.
Lent by The Downtown Gallery.

below:
Ad Reinhardt.
Abstract Painting. 1938.
Oil on canvas. 40½ x 38½.
Lent by Mrs. Rita Reinhardt.

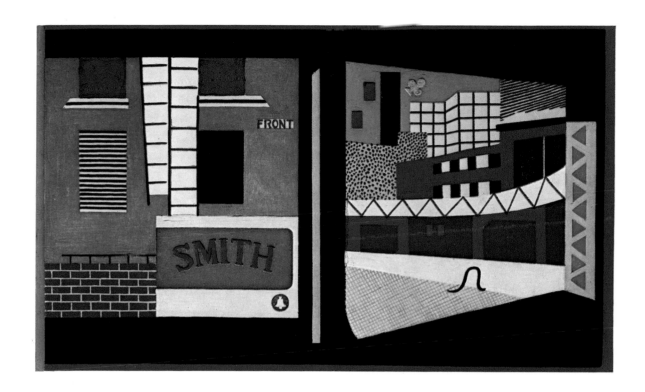

above:
Stuart Davis.
House and Street. 1931.
Oil on canvas. 26 x 42¼.
Collection Whitney Museum of American Art.

opposite:
Stuart Davis.
Swing Landscape. 1938.
Oil on canvas. 84 x 173½.
Lent by Indiana University Museum of Art,
    Extended loan from W.P.A. Federal Art Project.

above:
John Ferren.
Untitled. 1936.
Oil on canvas. 35 x 45¾.
Lent by the artist.

opposite:
Carl Holty.
Recording Angel. 1938.
Oil on composition board. 54 x 35½.
Lent by Graham Gallery Limited.

Expressionist Abstraction

opposite:
Milton Avery.
Vermont Hills. 1936.
Oil on canvas. 32 x 48.
Lent by Brandeis University Art Collection,
    Gift of William H. Weintraub, New York.

below:
Milton Avery.
Children at Sea Side. 1935.
Oil on canvas. 30 x 40.
Lent by Mrs. Milton Avery.

above:
Willem de Kooning.
Untitled Abstraction. c. 1931.
Oil on canvas. 23⅞ x 33.
Lent by the artist.

opposite:
Willem de Kooning.
Seated Man. c. 1939.
Oil on canvas. 38 x 34.
Lent by the artist.

right:
Hans Hofmann.
Abstract Figure. 1938.
Oil on plywood. 67½ x 43¾.
Lent by the Estate of the artist.

opposite:
Hans Hofmann.
Still Life, Yellow Table in Green. 1936.
Oil on plywood. 60 x 44½.
Lent by the Estate of the artist.

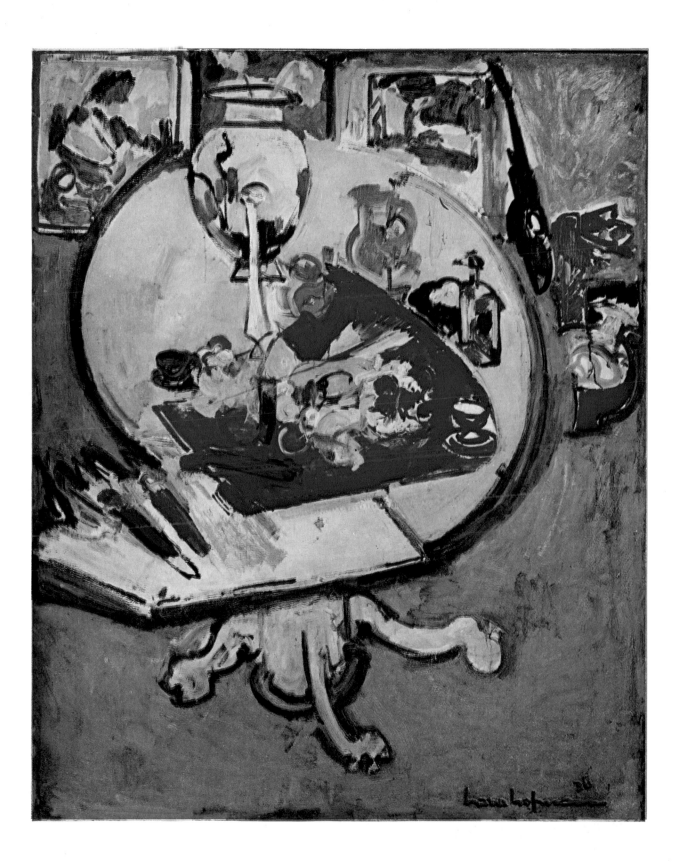

opposite:
Jackson Pollock.
The Flame. 1937.
Oil on canvas. 20⅛ x 30⅛.
Lent by Lee Krasner Pollock, courtesy of
    Marlborough-Gerson Gallery, New York.

left:
Mark Tobey.
Broadway Norm. 1935.
Tempera. 13⅝ x 9.
Lent by Mrs. Carol Ely Harper.

below:
Mark Tobey.
Cirque d'Hiver. 1933.
Pastel. 16⅞ x 21½.
Lent by Mr. and Mrs. Windsor Utley.

above:
Arshile Gorky.
The Artist and His Mother. c. 1926-36.
Oil on canvas. 60 x 50.
Collection Whitney Museum of American Art,
    Gift of Julien Levy for Maro and Natsha Gorky
    in memory of their father.

opposite:
Arshile Gorky.
Painting. 1936-37.
Oil on canvas. 38 x 48.
Collection Whitney Museum of American Art.

left:
Karl Knaths.
Maritime. 1931.
Oil on canvas. 40 x 32.
Lent by Mr. and Mrs. Laughlin Phillips.

opposite:
John D. Graham.
Vox Humana. 1931.
Oil and sand on canvas. 47 x 32.
Lent by Yale University Art Gallery,
   Gift of Collection Société Anonyme.

Sculpture

above:
Gaston Lachaise.
Dans La Nuit. 1935.
Bronze. 31 x 88½ x 41.
Private Collection, New York.

opposite:
Elie Nadelman.
Two Circus Women. c. 1930.
Papier maché. 61½ x 38 x 12.
Lent by Philip Johnson.

opposite:
David Smith.
Vertical Structure (Vertical Construction). 1939.
Steel with copper. 45⅞ x 33¼ x 22⅜.
Lent by The Estate of David Smith, courtesy of
    Marlborough-Gerson Gallery, New York.

below:
David Smith.
Untitled. (Reclining Figure). 1937.
Iron, painted aluminum. 23⅞ x 38¾ x 10⅝.
Lent by The Estate of David Smith, courtesy of
    Marlborough-Gerson Gallery, New York.

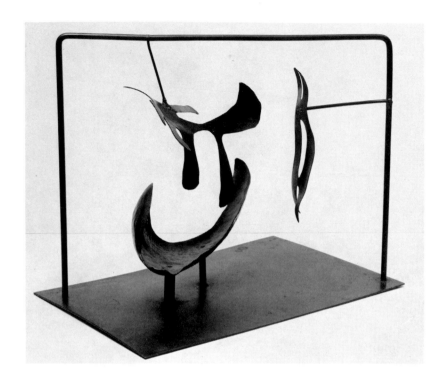

opposite:
Alexander Calder.
Whale. 1937 (remade 1964).
Stabile: Painted sheet metal. 68 x 69½ x 45⅜.
Lent by The Museum of Modern Art, New York,
  Gift of the artist, 1965.

left:
Ibram Lassaw.
Sculpture in Steel. 1938.
Steel. 18½ x 24 x 15.
Lent by the artist.

below:
José de Rivera.
Red and Black (Double Element). 1938.
Painted aluminum. 11½ x 16½ x 14½.
Lent by Mrs. Margarete Schultz.

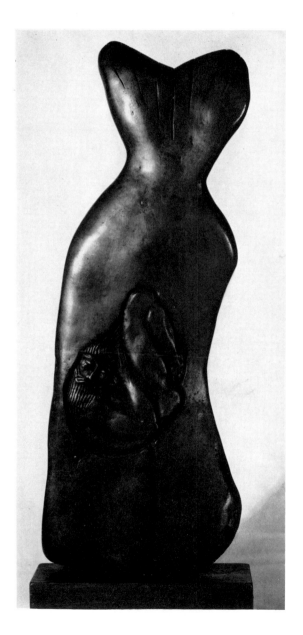

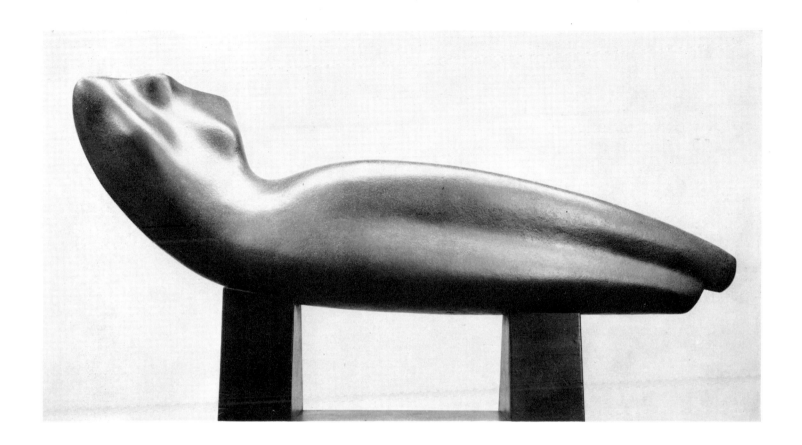

above:
Alexander Archipenko.
Torso in Space. 1936.
Metalized terra cotta. 18 x 60½ x 7½.
Collection Whitney Museum of American Art,
    Gift of Mr. and Mrs. Peter A. Rübel.

opposite left:
William Zorach.
Youth. 1935.
Borneo mahogany. 51½ x 14 x 10.
Lent by The Downtown Gallery.

opposite right:
John B. Flannagan.
Jonah and the Whale. 1937.
Bronze. 29½ x 11 x 3.
Lent by The Minneapolis Institute of Arts.

above:
Joseph Cornell.
Variété de Minéralogie. 1939.
Construction. 9¼ x 14¼ x 2.
Lent by James Merrill.

right:
John Storrs.
Composition Around Two Voids. 1932.
Stainless steel. 20 x 10 x 6.
Collection Whitney Museum of American Art,
    Gift of Monique Storrs Booz.

opposite:
Theodore Roszak.
Construction in White. 1937.
Wood, masonite, clear plastic. 80½ x 80½ x 12.
Lent by National Collection of Fine Arts,
    Smithsonian Institution.

Europeans in America

opposite:
Jean Hélion.
Figure Complexe. 1938.
Oil on canvas. 51⅝ x 69⅜.
Lent by Willard Gallery.

below:
Fernand Léger.
Composition with Aloes. 1935.
Oil on canvas. 44⅞ x 57½.
Lent by The Solomon R. Guggenheim Museum, New York.

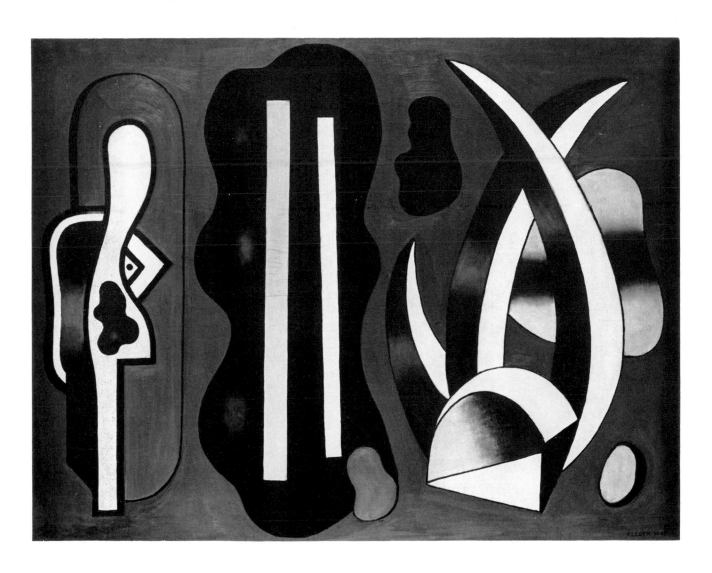

Yves Tanguy.
Le Temps Meuble. 1939.
Oil on canvas. 45⅞ x 35⅛.
Lent by James Thrall Soby.

Catalogue

Measurements are in inches, height preceding width and depth.

1 **Albers Josef.** b. 1888. To U.S. 1933.
Movement in Gray. 1939.
Oil on masonite. 36 x 35.
Lent by the artist.

2 **Albers, Josef.**
Equal and Unequal. 1939.
Oil on masonite. 19 x 43.
Lent by the artist.

3 **Albright, Ivan.** b. 1897.
And God Created Man in His Own Image.
1930-31.
Oil on canvas. 48 x 26.
Lent by the artist.

4 **Archipenko, Alexander.** (1887-1964).
Torso in Space. 1936.
Metalized terra cotta. 18 x 60½ x 7½.
Collection Whitney Museum of American Art,
Gift of Mr. and Mrs. Peter A. Rübel.

5 **Avery, Milton.** (1893-1965).
Children at Sea Side. 1935.
Oil on canvas. 30 x 40.
Lent by Mrs. Milton Avery.

6 **Avery, Milton.**
Vermont Hills. 1936.
Oil on canvas. 32 x 48.
Lent by Brandeis University Art Collection,
Gift of William H. Weintraub, New York.

7 **Benton, Thomas Hart.** b. 1889.
Cradling Wheat. 1938.
Oil on canvas. 31 x 38.
Lent by City Art Museum of St. Louis.

8 **Berman, Eugene.** b. 1899. To U.S. 1935.
The Gates of the City, Nightfall. 1937.
Oil on canvas. 30¼ x 40¼.
Lent by The Museum of Modern Art, New
York, Gift of James Thrall Soby, 1947.

9 **Bluemner, Oscar.** (1867-1938).
A Situation in Yellow. c. 1933.
Oil on canvas. 36 x 50½.
Collection Whitney Museum of American Art,
Gift of Mr. and Mrs. Harry L. Koenigsberg.

10 **Blume, Peter.** b. 1906.
The Eternal City. 1934-37.
Oil on canvas. 34 x 47⅞.
Lent by The Museum of Modern Art,
New York, Mrs. Simon Guggenheim Fund,
1942.

11 **Bolotowsky, Ilya.** b. 1907.
White Abstraction. 1934-35.
Oil on canvas. 36¾ x 19.
Lent by Grace Borgenicht Gallery.

12 **Bruce, Patrick Henry.** (1881-1936).*
Forms. c. 1929-30.
Oil on canvas. 23¼ x 36.
Lent by Benjamin F. Garber.

13 **Burchfield, Charles.** (1893-1967).
Black Iron. 1935.
Watercolor. 29 x 41.
Lent by Dr. and Mrs. Irving F. Burton.

14 **Burchfield, Charles.**
Old House by Creek. 1932-38.
Oil on canvas. 34½ x 57.
Collection Whitney Museum of American Art.

*Bruce's death has always been listed as 1937,
and has continued to be even though I published
the correct date in my *Synchromism and Color
Principles in American Painting, 1910-1930*
(New York: 1965). Bruce died in New York on
November 12, 1936, three months after his return
from Paris where he had lived and worked
since 1904. (Date verified by Certificate of Death
#24627, Department of Health, New York City
[borough of Manhattan].) The erroneous date can
be traced to a statement written by Henri-Pierre
Roché for the catalogue, *The Collection of the
Société Anonyme,* Yale University, (New Haven,
1950) in which Roché said that in the spring of
1937 he had learned that Bruce had died several
months earlier. Roché, however, did not state
that Bruce actually died in 1937, but that is the
date which has been used ever since.

15 **Calder, Alexander.** b. 1898.
The Rusty Bottle. c. 1936.
Sheet metal and wire. 96 h.
Lent by Perls Galleries, New York.

16 **Calder, Alexander.**
Whale. 1937 (remade 1964).
Stabile: Painted sheet metal. 68 x 69½ x
45⅜.
Lent by The Museum of Modern Art,
New York, Gift of the artist, 1965.

17 **Carles, Arthur B.** (1882-1952).
Abstract Still Life, Flowers. 1935.
Oil on canvas. 51½ x 41.
Lent by Graham Gallery Limited.

18 **Carles, Arthur B.**
Composition. 1937-40.
Oil on canvas. 54½ x 67.
Private Collection.

19 **Castellon, Fédérico.** b. 1914.
The Dark Figure. 1938.
Oil on canvas. 17 x 26⅛.
Collection Whitney Museum of American Art.

20 **Cavallon, Giorgio.** b. 1904.
Untitled. 1938-39.
Oil on canvas. 17 x 14.
Lent by the artist.

21 **Cornell, Joseph.** b. 1903.
Soap Bubble Set. 1939.
Construction. 14 x 9 x 2½.
Lent by Mr. and Mrs. E. A. Bergman.

22 **Cornell, Joseph.**
Variété de Minéralogie. 1939.
Construction. 9¼ x 14¼ x 2.
Lent by James Merrill.

23 **Crawford, Ralston.** b. 1906.
Maitland Bridge, Number 2. 1938.
Oil on canvas. 40 x 32.
Lent by William H. Lane Foundation.

24 **Curry, John Steuart.** (1897-1946).
Wisconsin Landscape. 1938-39.
Oil on canvas. 42 x 84.
Lent by The Metropolitan Museum of Art,
George A. Hearn Fund, 1942.

25 **Davis, Stuart.** (1894-1964).
House and Street. 1931.
Oil on canvas. 26 x 42¼.
Collection Whitney Museum of American Art.

26 **Davis, Stuart.**
Swing Landscape. 1938.
Oil on canvas. 84 x 173½.
Lent by Indiana University Museum of Art.
Extended loan from W.P.A. Federal Art
Project.

27 **Demuth, Charles.** (1883-1935).
Buildings, Lancaster. 1930.
Oil on composition board. 24 x 20.
Collection Whitney Museum of American Art,
Anonymous gift.

28 **Dickinson, Edwin.** b. 1891.
Finger Lakes. 1935.
Oil on canvas. 23½ x 28½.
Lent by Chauncey L. Waddell.

29 **Diller, Burgoyne.** (1906-1965).
First Theme. 1933-34.
Oil on canvas. 30 x 30.
Lent by Mrs. Burgoyne Diller.

30 **Diller, Burgoyne.**
Second Theme. 1938.
Oil on canvas. 34 x 34.
Lent by Mrs. Burgoyne Diller.

31 **Dove, Arthur G.** (1880-1946).
Ferry Boat Wreck. 1931.
Oil on canvas. 18 x 30.
Collection Whitney Museum of American Art,
Gift of Mr. and Mrs. Roy R. Neuberger
(and purchase).

32 **Dove, Arthur G.**
Sunrise, I. 1937.
Oil on canvas. 25 x 35.
Lent by William H. Lane Foundation.

33 **Evergood, Philip.** b. 1901.
Lily and the Sparrows. 1939.
Oil on composition board. 30 x 24.
Collection Whitney Museum of American Art.

34 **Ferren, John.** b. 1905.
Untitled. 1936.
Oil on canvas. 35 x 45¾.
Lent by the artist.

35 **Flannagan, John B.** (1895-1942).
Jonah and the Whale. 1937.
Bronze. 29½ x 11 x 3.
Lent by The Minneapolis Institute of Arts.

36 **Friedman, Arnold.** (1879-1946).
    Hudson River. 1936.
    Oil on canvas. 30 x 25.
    Lent by Mr. and Mrs. Baltus B.
        Van Kleeck, Jr.

37 **Glarner, Fritz.** b. 1899.
    Painting. 1937.
    Oil on canvas. 45 x 56.
    Lent by the artist.

38 **Gorky, Arshile.** (1904-1948).
    The Artist and His Mother. c. 1926-36.
    Oil on canvas. 60 x 50.
    Collection Whitney Museum of American Art,
        Gift of Julien Levy for Maro and Natsha
        Gorky in memory of their father.

39 **Gorky, Arshile.**
    Painting. 1936-37.
    Oil on canvas. 38 x 48.
    Collection Whitney Museum of American Art.

40 **Graham, John D.** (1887-1961).
    Vox Humana. 1931.
    Oil and sand on canvas. 47 x 32.
    Lent by Yale University Art Gallery, Gift of
        Collection Société Anonyme.

41 **Graham, John D.**
    The Embrace. 1932.
    Oil and sand on canvas. 36 x 29.
    Lent by Dorothy Dehner.

42 **Graves, Morris.** b. 1910.
    Bird in the Mist. 1937.
    Tempera. 30½ x 27.
    Lent by Mr. and Mrs. Roy R. Neuberger.

43 **Greene, Balcomb.** b. 1904.
    Green Composition. 1938.
    Oil on masonite. 14½ x 22½.
    Lent by the artist.

44 **Gropper, William.** b. 1897.
    Art Patrons. 1939.
    Oil on canvas. 15¼ x 21¾.
    Lent by City Art Museum of St. Louis.

45 **Grosz, George.** (1893-1959).
    Nazi Justice. 1937.
    Watercolor and ink on paper. 19⅜ x 25.
    Lent by High Museum Art Association.

46 **Grosz, George.**
    A Piece of My World, II. c. 1938.
    Oil on canvas. 39½ x 65.
    Lent by the Estate of George Grosz.

47 **Guglielmi, Louis.** (1906-1956).
    Isaac Walton in Brooklyn. 1937.
    Oil on composition board. 29¾ x 23⅞.
    Lent by The Museum of Modern Art,
        Extended loan from the United States
        W.P.A. Art Program, 1939.

48 **Hartley, Marsden.** (1877-1943).
    Eight Bells' Folly: Memorial for Hart Crane.
        1933.
    Oil on canvas. 31⅝ x 39⅜.
    Lent by University of Minnesota Art Gallery,
        Gift of Ione and Hudson D. Walker, 1960.

49 **Hartley, Marsden.**
    *Rising Wave, Indian Point, Georgetown,
        Maine.* 1937-38.
    Oil on board. 22 x 28.
    Lent by The Baltimore Museum of Art,
        Edward Joseph Gallagher III Memorial
        Collection.

50 **Hélion, Jean.** b. 1904. In U.S. 1936-1940.
    Figure Complexe. 1938.
    Oil on canvas. 51⅝ x 69⅜.
    Lent by Willard Gallery.

51 **Hofmann, Hans.** (1880-1966).
    Still Life, Yellow Table in Green. 1936.
    Oil on plywood. 60 x 44½.
    Lent by the Estate of the artist.

52 **Hofmann, Hans.**
    Abstract Figure. 1938.
    Oil on plywood. 67½ x 43¾.
    Lent by the Estate of the artist.

53 **Holty, Carl.** b. 1900.
    Recording Angel. 1938.
    Oil on composition board. 54 x 35½.
    Lent by Graham Gallery Limited.

54 **Holtzman, Harry.** b. 1912.
    Vertical Volume, Number 1. 1939-40.
    Oil and casein on gesso on masonite.
        60 x 12.
    Lent by the artist.

55 **Hopper, Edward.** (1882-1967).
    Early Sunday Morning. 1930.
    Oil on canvas. 35 x 60.
    Collection Whitney Museum of American Art.

56 **Hopper, Edward.**
    New York Movie. 1939.
    Oil on canvas. 32¼ x 40⅛.
    Lent by The Museum of Modern Art,
        New York, Given anonymously, 1941.

57 **Joe Jones.** (1909-1963).
American Farm. 1936.
Oil and tempera on canvas. 30 x 40.
Collection Whitney Museum of American Art.

58 **Knaths, Karl.** b. 1891.
Maritime. 1931.
Oil on canvas. 40 x 32.
Lent by Mr. and Mrs. Laughlin Phillips.

59 **de Kooning, Willem.** b. 1904.
Untitled Abstraction. c. 1931.
Oil on canvas. 23⅞ x 33.
Lent by the artist.

60 **de Kooning, Willem.**
Seated Man. c. 1939.
Oil on canvas. 38 x 34.
Lent by the artist.

61 **Kuhn, Walt.** (1877-1949).
The Blue Clown. 1931.
Oil on canvas. 30 x 25.
Collection Whitney Museum of American Art.

62 **Kuniyoshi, Yasuo.** (1890-1953).
I'm Tired. 1938.
Oil on canvas. 40¼ x 31.
Collection Whitney Museum of American Art.

63 **Lachaise, Gaston.** (1882-1935).
Dans La Nuit. 1935.
Bronze. 31 x 88½ x 41.
Private Collection, New York.

64 **Lassaw, Ibram.** b. 1913.
Sculpture in Steel. 1938.
Steel. 18½ x 24 x 15.
Lent by the artist.

65 **Léger, Fernand.** (1881-1955). In U.S. 1931,
1935, 1938-39, 1940-46.
Composition with Aloes. 1935.
Oil on canvas. 44⅞ x 57½.
Lent by The Solomon R. Guggenheim
Museum, New York.

66 **Levine, Jack.** b. 1915.
String Quartette. 1934-37.
Tempera and oil on composition board.
47½ x 67½.
Lent by The Metropolitan Museum of Art,
Arthur H. Hearn Fund, 1942.

67 **Man Ray.** b. 1890.
Observatory Time — The Lovers. 1932-34.
Oil on canvas. 39⅜ x 98½.
Lent by William N. Copley.

68 **Man Ray.**
Le Beau Temps. 1939.
Oil on canvas. 112 x 108.
Lent by Cordier & Ekstrom, Inc.

69 **Marin, John.** (1870-1953).
Region of Brooklyn Bridge Fantasy. 1932.
Watercolor. 18¾ x 22¼.
Collection Whitney Museum of American Art.

70 **Marin, John.**
Sea After Hurricane, Cape Split, Maine.
1938.
Oil on canvas. 23 x 30.
Lent by San Francisco Museum of Art,
Gift of Mrs. Henry Potter Russell.

71 **Marsh, Reginald.** (1898-1954).
Twenty-Cent Movie. 1936.
Egg tempera on composition board. 30 x 40.
Collection Whitney Museum of American Art.

72 **Marsh, Reginald.**
Human Pool Tables. 1938.
Egg tempera on composition board.
29¾ x 40.
Collection Whitney Museum of American Art,
Gift of Mrs. Reginald Marsh and
William Benton.

73 **Matta (Sebastian Antonio Matta Euchaurren).**
b. 1912. In U.S. 1939-48.
Prescience. 1939.
Oil on canvas. 36 x 52⅟₁₆.
Lent by Wadsworth Atheneum, Hartford:
The Ella Gallup Sumner and Mary Catlin
Sumner Collection.

74 **Maurer, Alfred H.** (1868-1932).
Twin Heads. c. 1930.
Oil on canvas. 26⅜ x 18.
Collection Whitney Museum of American Art,
Gift of Mr. and Mrs. Hudson D. Walker
(and exchange).

75 **McNeil, George.** b. 1908.
Green Forms Dominant. 1938-39.
Tempera on gesso panel. 20 x 24.
Lent by the artist.

76 **Moholy-Nagy, László.** (1895-1946).
Space Modulator. 1938-40.
Oil on canvas. 47 x 47.
Collection Whitney Museum of American Art,
Gift of Mrs. Sibyl Moholy-Nagy.

77 **Morris, George L. K.** b. 1905.
Stockbridge Church. 1935.
Oil on canvas. 54 x 45.
Lent by The Downtown Gallery.

78 **Nadelman, Elie.** (1882-1946).
Two Circus Women. c. 1930.
Papier maché. 61½ x 38 x 12.
Lent by Philip Johnson.

79 **O'Keeffe, Georgia.** b. 1887.
Black, White and Blue. 1930.
Oil on canvas. 48 x 30.
Lent by The Downtown Gallery Collection.

80 **O'Keeffe, Georgia.**
Deer's Skull with Pedernal. 1936.
Oil on canvas. 36 x 30.
Lent by William H. Lane Foundation.

81 **Pollock, Jackson.** (1912-1956).
Birth. 1937.
Oil on canvas. 46 x 22.
Lent by Lee Krasner Pollock, courtesy of
Marlborough-Gerson Gallery, New York.

82 **Pollock, Jackson.**
The Flame. 1937.
Oil on canvas. 20⅛ x 30⅛.
Lent by Lee Krasner Pollock, courtesy of
Marlborough-Gerson Gallery, New York.

83 **Reinhardt, Ad.** (1913-1967).
Abstract Painting. 1938.
Oil on canvas. 40½ x 38½.
Lent by Mrs. Rita Reinhardt.

84 **de Rivera, José.** b. 1904.
Red and Black (Double Element). 1938.
Painted aluminum. 11½ x 16½ x 14½.
Lent by Mrs. Margarete Schultz.

85 **Robus, Hugo.** (1885-1964).
Dawn. 1933.
Bronze. 66½ x 25 x 22.
Lent by Forum Gallery.

86 **Roszak, Theodore.** b. 1907.
Construction in White. 1937.
Wood, masonite, clear plastic. 80½ x 80½
x 12.
Lent by National Collection of Fine Arts,
Smithsonian Institution.

87 **Sage, Kay.** (1898-1963).
My Room Has Two Doors. 1939.
Oil on canvas. 39 x 32.
Lent by The Mattatuck Museum.

88 **Shahn, Ben.** b. 1898.
The Passion of Sacco and Vanzetti. 1931-32.
From the Sacco-Vanzetti series of 23
paintings. Tempera on canvas. 84½ x 48.
Collection Whitney Museum of American Art,
Gift of Edith and Milton Lowenthal
in memory of Juliana Force.

89 **Shahn, Ben.**
Scotts Run, West Virginia. 1937.
Tempera on cardboard. 22¼ x 27⅞.
Collection Whitney Museum of American Art.

90 **Sheeler, Charles.** (1883-1965).
River Rouge Plant. 1932.
Oil on canvas. 20 x 24⅛.
Collection Whitney Museum of American Art.

91 **Sheeler, Charles.**
Clapboards. 1937.
Oil on canvas. 21 x 19½.
Lent by The Pennsylvania Academy of the
Fine Arts.

92 **Smith, David.** (1906-1965).
Untitled. (Reclining Figure.) 1937.
Iron, painted aluminum. 23⅞ x 38¾ x
10⅝.
Lent by The Estate of David Smith, courtesy
of Marlborough-Gerson Gallery, New York.

93 **Smith, David.**
Vertical Structure (Vertical Construction).
1939.
Steel with copper. 45⅞ x 33¼ x 22⅜.
Lent by The Estate of David Smith, courtesy
of Marlborough-Gerson Gallery, New York.

94 **Soyer, Raphael.** b. 1899.
The Flower Vendor. 1935. (Repainted 1940.)
Oil on canvas. 30 x 36.
Lent by Emil J. Arnold.

95 **Stella, Joseph.** (1877-1946).
Bird and Tree. c. 1938-40.
Oil on canvas. 53 x 32.
Lent by the Stella Estate, courtesy of Robert
Schoelkopf Gallery, New York.

96 **Storrs, John.** (1885-1956).
Abstract I. 1932.
Oil on canvas. 58 x 45.
Lent by The Downtown Gallery.

97 **Storrs, John.**
 Composition Around Two Voids. 1932.
 Stainless steel. 20 x 10 x 6.
 Collection Whitney Museum of American Art,
  Gift of Monique Storrs Booz.

98 **Tack, Augustus Vincent.** (1870-1949).
 Before Egypt. c. 1930-35.
 Oil on canvas mounted on composition
  board.
   Canvas: 16¾ x 36½; board: 20 x 45.
 Collection Whitney Museum of American Art,
  Gift of Duncan Phillips.

99 **Tanguy, Yves.** (1900-1955). To U.S. 1939.
 Le Temps Meuble. 1939.
 Oil on canvas. 45⅞ x 35⅛.
 Lent by James Thrall Soby.

100 **Tchelitchew, Pavel.** (1898-1957). In U.S.
  1934, 1938-48.
 Whirlwind. 1939.
 Oil on canvas. 28½ x 23¾.
 Lent by The Metropolitan Museum of Art,
  Arthur H. Hearn Fund, 1950.

101 **Tobey, Mark.** b. 1890.
 Cirque d'Hiver. 1933.
 Pastel. 16⅞ x 21½.
 Lent by Mr. and Mrs. Windsor Utley.

102 **Tobey, Mark.**
 Broadway Norm. 1935.
 Tempera. 13⅝ x 9.
 Lent by Mrs. Carol Ely Harper.

103 **Walkowitz, Abraham.** (1880-1965).
 From My Window. 1930.
 Oil on canvas. 40¼ x 26.
 Collection Whitney Museum of American Art,
  Gift of the artist in memory of Gertrude
  V. Whitney.

104 **Wood, Grant.** (1892-1942).
 Daughters of Revolution. 1932.
 Oil on panel. 20 x 40.
 Lent by Cincinnati Art Museum.

105 **Xceron, Jean.** (1890-1967).
 Composition Number 242. 1937.
 Oil on canvas. 45⅞ x 31⅞.
 Lent by The Solomon R. Guggenheim
  Museum, New York.

106 **Zorach, William.** (1887-1966).
 Youth. 1935.
 Borneo mahogany. 51½ x 14 x 10.
 Lent by The Downtown Gallery.

Selected Bibliography

The Bibliography is by no means intended as exhaustive. It is rather a listing of those studies which the author consulted and found most instructive out of a mammoth literature covering the entire decade. More specialized and extensive bibliographies can be found in those works so noted. Monographs on individual artists are listed only when they contain discussions which are particularly relevant to the present study of the 1930's.

Manuscript Collections

Archives of American Art, Detroit and New York
Documents of the Government Art Projects, 1933-43.
Individual Collections: Artists, Collectors, Critics, Historians, Government officials.
Tape Recorded Interviews: Artists, Government officials.

Columbia Oral History Collection, Columbia University, New York
Interviews with artists, government officials, writers and others involved with the 1930's.

Franklin D. Roosevelt MSS., Franklin D. Roosevelt Library, Hyde Park, New York
Roosevelt correspondence includes items from artists, officials and others bearing on government and public attitudes toward the arts in the 1930's.

Alfred Stieglitz MSS., American Literature Collection, Yale University
A rich fund of correspondence from literally hundreds of artists and others connected with the arts which bears on the many currents of the period.

Whitney Museum of American Art, New York
Documents on individual artists and other aspects of the 1930's.

Social, Political and Intellectual History

Aaron, Daniel. *Writers on The Left.* New York, 1965.

Beard, Charles and Mary. *America in Midpassage.* 2 vols. New York, 1939.

Bernstein, Irving. *The Lean Years.* Boston, 1960.

Clurman, Harold. *The Fervent Years.* New York, 1957.

Cooke, Alistair. *A Generation on Trial.* New York, 1958.

Cowley, Malcolm. *Exile's Return: Narrative of Ideas.* New York, 1934.

Geismar, Maxwell. *Writers in Crisis.* Boston, 1942.

Gurke, Leo. *The Angry Decade.* New York, 1947.

Howe, Irving, and Coser, Lewis. *The American Communist Party.* Boston, 1957.

Josephson, Matthew. *Infidel in The Temple: A Memoir of The 1930's.* New York, 1967.

Kazin, Alfred. *On Native Grounds: An Interpretation of Modern American Prose Literature.* New York, 1942.

Kempton, Murray. *Part of Our Time.* New York, 1955.

Leuchtenberg, William E. *Franklin D. Roosevelt and The New Deal.* New York, 1963. Contains an extensive bibliography on all aspects of the 1930's, except the arts.

Lynd, Robert and Helen. *Middletown in Transition.* New York, 1937.

Orton, William Aylott. *America in Search of Culture.* Boston, 1933.

Ransom, John Crowe. *The New Criticism.* Norfolk, 1941.

Schlesinger, Arthur M., Jr. *The Age of Roosevelt.* 3 vols. Boston, 1957-60.

Wilson, Edmund. *The American Earthquake.* New York, 1958.

General Histories of Twentieth-Century Art

(With discussions of the 1930's. Does not include histories written during the period which reflect attitudes of the time.)

Baur, John I. H. *Revolution and Tradition in Modern American Art.* Cambridge, 1951.

Geldzahler, Henry. *American Painting in the 20th Century.* New York, The Metropolitan Museum of Art, 1965. Bibliography of monographs on individual artists.

Goodrich, Lloyd, and Baur, John I. H. *American Art of Our Century.* New York, Whitney Museum of American Art, 1961.

Hunter, Sam. *Modern American Painting and Sculpture.* New York, 1959.

Rose, Barbara. *American Art Since 1900: A Critical History.* New York, 1967.

Studies Directly Related to the Art of the 1930's

Magazines.

In addition to specific articles cited in the bibliography, the following magazines should be consulted extensively and consecutively for a detailed knowledge of the events and issues most important to the 1930's. Dates in parentheses indicate the date of founding and where applicable, the date of the last issue. Unless otherwise indicated, the magazines span the entire decade.

American Magazine of Art. (Last issue: August, 1936.)

Art Digest.

Art Front. (November, 1934-December, 1937.)

Art News.

Bulletin of the Museum of Modern Art. (June, 1933.)

Cahiers d'Art.

Creative Art. (Last issue: May, 1933. Merged into *American Magazine of Art.*)

Magazine of Art. (Absorbed *Creative Art* and *American Magazine of Art.*)

New Masses.

New York Artist. (March-August, 1940.)

Partisan Review. (February, 1934.)

Exhibition Catalogues

Abstract Painting in America. New York: Whitney Museum of American Art, 1935.

American Abstract Artists. New York: 1937—. Catalogues of Annual Exhibitions. See especially 1938 and 1939 catalogues which include statements by George L. K. Morris, Ibram Lassaw, Balcomb Greene, Harry Holtzman and Albert Swinden.

Barr, Alfred H., Jr. *Cubism and Abstract Art.* New York: The Museum of Modern Art, 1936.

————. *Fantastic Art, Dada and Surrealism.* New York: The Museum of Modern Art, 1936.

Cahill, Holger. *American Art Today.* New York World's Fair, 1939.

————. *New Horizons in American Art.* New York: The Museum of Modern Art, 1936.

Denby, Edwin. *The 1930's: Painting in New York.* New York: Poindexter Gallery, 1957.

Gurin, Ruth. *American Abstract Artists, 1936-1966.* New York: The Riverside Museum, 1966.

Kirstein, Lincoln, and Levy, Julien. *Murals by American Painters and Photographers.* New York: The Museum of Modern Art, 1932.

Miller, Dorothy C., and Barr, Alfred H. Jr. (eds.). *American Realists and Magic Realists.* New York: The Museum of Modern Art, 1943.

Morris, George L. K. *American Abstract Art.* New York: Galerie St. Etienne, 1940.

O'Connor, Francis V. *Federal Art Patronage, 1933-1943.* College Park, Maryland, 1966. Extensive bibliography on the government art projects.

Books and Articles

Abell, Walter. "The Limits of Abstraction," *Magazine of Art.* XXVIII: D 1935.

Baigell, Matthew. "The Beginnings of 'The American Wave' and the Depression," *Art Journal.* XXVII: Summer 1968.

Baldinger, W. S. "Formal Change in Recent American Painting," *Art Bulletin.* XIX: D 1937.

Barzun, Jacques. "The Arts, The Snobs and The Democrat," *Of Human Freedom.* Boston, New York, 1939. (Reprinted in Philipson, M., *Aesthetics Today.* Cleveland, New York, 1961.)

Benton, Thomas H. *An Artist in America.* New York, 1937. (Revised edition, 1951.)

Blume, Peter. "After Surrealism," *The New Republic.* LXXX: O 1934.

Boswell, Peyton. *Modern American Painting.* New York, 1939.

Bruce, Edward, and Watson, Forbes. *Mural Designs, 1934-36.* Washington, D. C., Art in Federal Buildings, Inc., 1936.

Cahill, Holger, and Barr, Alfred H., Jr. (eds.). *Art in America, A Complete Survey*. New York, 1935.

————. *Art in America in Modern Times*. New York, 1934.

Campbell, Lawrence. "Paintings from WPA," *Art News*. S 1961.

Craven, Thomas. *Men of Art*. New York, 1934.

————. *Modern Art—The Men, The Movements, The Meaning*. New York, 1934.

————. *Thomas Hart Benton*. New York, 1939.

————. "Naturalism in Art," *Forum*. XCV: J-Je 1936.

————. "The Curse of French Culture," *Forum*. LXXXII: Jl 1929.

————. "Men of Art: American Style," *The American Mercury*. 6: D 1925.

Davis, Stuart. "Abstract Painting," *Art of Today*. Ap 1935.

————. "Arshile Gorky, in the 1930's, A Personal Recollection," *Magazine of Art*. XLIV: F 1951.

————. "Abstract Art in the American Scene," *Parnassus*. XIII: Mr 1941.

Duffus, R. L. *The American Renaissance*. New York, 1928.

Gallatin, A. E. *Museum of Living Art*. New York, 1940.

Gallatin, A. E., Morris, George L. K., and Tauber-Arp, Sophie, (eds.). *Plastique*. (Paris) 3: 1938. (Special number dedicated to American Art.)

Geist, Sidney. "Prelude: The 1930's," *Arts*. XXX: S 1956.

Gorky, Arshile. "Stuart Davis," *Creative Art*. IX: S 1931.

Graham, John D. *System and Dialectics of Art*. New York, 1937.

————. "Primitive Art and Picasso," *Magazine of Art*. 30: Ap 1937.

Greenberg, Clement. "The Late Thirties in New York," 1957. (Reprinted in *Art and Culture*. Boston, 1961.)

————. "New York Painting Only Yesterday," *Art News*. Summer 1957.

Hofmann, Hans. "Painting and Culture," *Fortnightly*, S 1931. (Reprinted in Hofmann, *Search for The Real And Other Essays*. Cambridge, Massachusetts, 1967.)

Janis, Sidney. *Abstract and Surrealist Art in America*. New York, 1944.

Jansen, H. W. "The International Aspects of Regionalism," *College Art Journal*. 2: My, 1943.

Jewell, Edwin A. *Have We An American Art?* New York, 1943.

Kootz, Samuel. *Modern American Painters*. New York, 1930.

————. *New Frontiers in American Painting*. New York, 1943.

Krasner, Lee. "Jackson Pollock, an interview with L. Krasner" (by B. Glaser). *Arts*. XLI: Ap 1967.

Larkin, Oliver W. *Art and Life in America*. New York, 1949.

Martin, J. R. "Marxism and The History of Art," *College Art Journal*. 11: 1951.

Mellquist, Jerome. *The Emergence of an American Art*. New York, 1942.

Morris, George L. K. "To the American Abstract Artists," *Partisan Review*. Mr 1938.

Morris, George L. K., and Kirstein, Lincoln. "Life or Death for Abstract Art?," *Magazine of Art*. XXXVI: Mr 1943.

Motherwell, Robert. "The Modern Painter's World," *Dyn*. VI: 1944.

Neuhaus, Eugen. *The History and Ideals of American Art*. Stanford, California, 1931.

Pearson, Ralph. "The Failure of the Art Critics," *Forum and Century*. XCIV: N-Ja 1936.

Schapiro, Meyer. "Nature of Abstract Art," *Marxist Quarterly*. I: Ja-Mr 1937.

————. "Populist Realism," *Partisan Review*. IV: D-My 1938.

[Simon, Sidney.] "Concerning the Beginnings of the New York School: 1939-1943. An Interview with Peter Busa and Matta, Conducted by Sidney Simon in Minneapolis in December, 1966." *Art International*. XI/6: Summer, 1967.

————. "Concerning the Beginnings of the New York School: 1939-43. An Interview with Robert Motherwell, Conducted by Sidney Simon in New York in January, 1967." *Ibid*.

Soby, James Thrall. *After Picasso*. Hartford, New York, 1935.

Sweeney, James J. *Plastic Redirections in Twentieth Century Painting*. Chicago, 1934.

Watson, Forbes. *American Painting Today*. Washington, 1939.